Life's Purpose

Development of Your Living and Eternal Spirit

Halim Ozkaptan Ph.D.

ISBN 978-0-6151-8403-6

Version 4

Cover Picture: "Cape Canaveral Sunrise" photographed by
Dr. William Swart

This book can be purchased at
www.lulu.com/content/1689005

Dedication

Elinor

Marriage represents hope and a promise. We have realized that hope and promise together. You have been steadfast in your love and devotion. You have taught me the true meaning of love and charity. You have placed no conditions on me and never asked anything for yourself. You are unquestioning and calm in difficult times and when we are in dangerous situations. You have raised four beautiful children with love and cheerfulness. You express goodwill for everyone that you meet. You are as beautiful to me as the day we met. I love you as much today as the passion that led to our marriage.

Oz

Acknowledgement

I wish to acknowledge and thank my friends, present and departed, for their gifts of friendship and for having enriched my life. I also wish to thank the many people who have extended good will, support when in need, and who opened doors when they were closed.

I acknowledge the many books, read over a lifetime, that have contributed to my thoughts. Most notably, they are the major religious texts, and books by James Campbell, Jane Roberts, and Elsa Barker.

Preface

Many people have had insights and thoughts beyond their normal experiences, as well as moments of revelation and awe. As the pressures of earning a living, raising a family and dealing with daily problems diminish, these moments increase. One also has more time to contemplate the miracle of life. These are the thoughts that I have put down.

Are they all my original thoughts? No. They include what I have gained from the books and articles that I have read and from conversations with my friends. They also represent insights and reflections on the many challenges and experiences of a lifetime. Many of the thoughts came through a "stream of consciousness" and inspiration.

For ease of expression, this book is written in the first person as "God." It has put off some people. However, it is not intended to be presumptuous. It was only a much easier way to express the thoughts in this book.

Introduction

Prepared by

Dr. Kent Williams, Professor, University of Central Florida

The "Transcendent Self" is the term applied by the noted psychoanalytic theorist Carl Jung to describe the psychic force which is rarely actualized and expressed by individuals but which is inherent in all mankind. It describes the wisdom which is characteristic of major religious figures and philosophers throughout history. It can be likened to a Zen state of mind whereby ones lifelong experiences emerge to form a new state of consciousness beyond the boundaries of current social cognition. This is the state of mind which generated the text which follows. It is integration, better yet a harmony, of various beliefs about notions of morality, religion and social governance. Dr Ozkaptan entangles ideas from Christianity, Islam, evolutionary psychology, psychoanalytic theory, and mythology to present a set of principles to live by consistent with transcendence, much akin to a Course in Miracles and the Seth books, yet more palatable for our times. It is a refreshing break from our digital, mechanistic way of thinking about why we are here. It personifies the emergent nature of our universe and the self organizing forces which strive to give order to chaos. Ozkaptan gives hope for the preservation of the mysteries of living by the eternal spirit which resides within all of us.

Table of Contents

Chapter 1

God Speaks

To those who want to know, to those who are willing to listen and to those who are willing to suspend their disbelief, I speak. Who am I? I am the Living and Eternal Spirit that created you. I created and continue to permeate and sustain the universe with my spirit. My essence is love. My message to you is that you are also a part of my living and eternal spirit. Your living spirit is eternal, although your physical body will perish in time.

You are a part of my living and eternal sprit.

Many times you may have asked, "Why am I here? What is the meaning and purpose of life? Am I powerless in the face of random events? Is there evil? Why do bad things

1

happen?" You have also marveled at the majesty of the world and the very nature of human existence. Is it an accident? Are you an accident and at the mercy of forces beyond your control?

I will try to answer these questions and others that you may have. You may never fully accept what I say. However, the following will help you to gain some understanding concerning your purpose on earth and about your spiritual self. One day, it will become gloriously clear.

The power of my spirit in you provides you with enormous powers of creativity and free choice. However, your free choice can lead you astray. Your purpose on earth is to control this power, and by doing so, to grow and to become part of me in love.

You unknowingly interact with your inner spirit at every moment of your life. Every one of your actions is weighed against it as a deficit or gain in your spiritual growth and moral worth. I will explain the meaning and impact of your spiritual self on your daily life in the following sections.

The essence of my spirit is love.

Chapter 2

Creation of Your World

Many scientists think that the world and the life upon it is a miraculous accident. They think that man emerged from some primal organism that crawled out of the slime and somehow managed its own development into a complex organism with a sense of sight, hearing, taste, emotion and reason.

Do you really believe that the diversity, finely balanced and flawless interdependence and beauty of the world are an accident or a random occurrence? Do you really think that the air you breathe, the water you depend upon and the sun that warms you happened by chance? Can you imagine a better and more perfect creation?

Some of your scientists also believe that your consciousness derives from your body. How could such a presumed accidental organism, a piece of flesh, possess consciousness, thought or even love? Your consciousness is part of my living and eternal spirit. It is not the result of one's body or flesh. It is the cause of life as you know it.

As I imagined you, I created you with my consciousness. I distributed sparks of myself that became you. Your consciousness derives from and is part of my spirit that is within you. It is your consciousness that creates your body and sustains it at every moment. It propels your thoughts and sustains you in every instance. You could not see, hear or think without my spirit and the consciousness that emanates through your body. Your flesh is only a vehicle for these functions and does not create them.

I imagined you and the world and dispersed portions of myself, my spirit, and my consciousness to form and create your reality.

As I imagined the components of the world, I dispersed my consciousness and created them. I created a perfect world. I also gave you the means with which to sustain your life on earth. The food you eat, the lumber that you use to build your homes were imagined and created by me.

Each individual at their birth is essentially a rough sketch based upon the experiences of a previous lifetime. Your specific personality, the "you" that you become, is developed through the creativity endowed in your consciousness.

In a manner of speaking, you flesh and develop yourself through your own thoughts and beliefs. Like an artist, you add the color and details to the rough sketch that you are born with.[1] You develop yourself into the person that you are through the power of your consciousness and beliefs. Thus you are a part of me and endowed by my creativity. I am everywhere as part of you, and you are everywhere as part of me.

Your consciousness creates your body, propels your thoughts and sustains you in every instance.

Each and every living thing shares a portion of my consciousness. Through my consciousness, my creativity continues as life manifests itself. It is for this reason that

---

[1] Roberts, J. (1994). <u>The Nature of Personal Reality.</u> Novato, Calif:New World Library.

consciousness is the basis of the world from which all living things are and were derived. This process continues today in your creation and recreation at every moment. My creativity abounds in the world and is perpetuated by your own creations as you are a part of me and my consciousness.

I am everywhere as part of my children and you are everywhere as part of me.

Consciousness creates the elements of flesh just as water is created from the oxygen and hydrogen in the air. As water becomes vapor, your consciousness continues after what you call death. As plants draw power from the sun, your body draws power from my spirit. My spirit is in every baby's smile, every person's tears and your laughter. You are not flesh alone.

Consciousness is not the final result; it is the cause of life as you know it.

I created a gene structure to guide evolution and to enable your adaptation to changing environments over the centuries. The gene structure also allows experimentation to create the myriad of life forms that abound on the earth. As you strive to develop your spirits so do your bodies adapt to changing environments.

Some scientists assert that evolution is proof that I do not exist. Yet, I create and guide evolution. Their ability to doubt is proof enough of my existence. The love between two people, such as a mother's love for her child, is proof that I exist. Love derives from my living and eternal spirit that is part of you. The doubters of my existence come from a sperm drop and deny my existence. They cannot explain your feelings of shame and free choice.

They come from a sperm drop and become loud disputers of my existence.

The capability of genes to evolve is part of my plan. It is easier for them to believe that genes are self organizing than to believe in my existence. Reason or scientific thought does not contradict your faith. I have given you reason to have faith. There is no conflict between faith and reason. Faith is rational. It is irrational to believe otherwise.

Your reason is the foundation of your faith.

I created a wide variety of mammals from sheep, horses, and cattle to whales and man. Yet you did not derive or descend from a common ancestor, but your physiology is the same! The similarity of physiology in such a large variety of mammals could not have occurred by chance. It is I, who developed the diversity of mammals with the same physiological structure as I did with other diverse species. How could the diversity of different mammals have the same physiological structure by chance? You are all my creations from the template of my design.

You are my creations from the template of my design.

My living and eternal spirit exists through you and my creations. My spirit permeates your world and universe and is pervasive. I do not exist as a separate and isolated being. I exist as a part of my creations and as the guiding spirit of the universe.

I am an integral part of your reality and existence.

I evolved as a spontaneous self organizing entity from the power and energy of the cosmos. I am the organizing and unifying force that gives structure and order to the universe at each level of organization down to its lowest level. My living and eternal spirit empowers the universe. Why did I create the world? I wanted to share my spirit, love and creativity. As I imagined you, I created you.

My spirit permeates your world and universe and is pervasive.

Chapter 3

Your Living and Eternal Spirit

Your spirit is and always will be, because it emanates from and is part of my spirit. Your lifetime is but a day for your immortal spirit. Immortality presupposes no beginning and no end. Your spirit like mine will exist for eternity. Your immediate life is but a passage in an endless journey. There is no time. As you cycle between earth and my presence, you will learn that "one day is a thousand years and a thousand years is but one day".[2]

One day is a thousand years and a thousand years is but a day.

---

[2] Barker, E. (1919). Letters From the Living Dead Man. NY: Mitchell Kennerley

Your living and eternal spirit is a reality, not hope or theory. It has the power to lighten your hearts, burdens and to give you freedom from sickness, hate and despair. It is the basis of love, hope and happiness. It is the foundation of your religion. If you believe that you are an accident of nature; that life is short, brutal and for the survival of the fittest; that old age is one of decay and that death is final; so shall it be. You will live with a veil over your eyes and will view life darkly. Your happiness and prosperity will be limited and subject to the random forces about you. You will be like a rudderless ship in the ocean subject to its forces. You will pass over to my side unprepared and in confusion.

However, if you are aware of your living and eternal spirit, and seek its development, you will be sustained by its vitality and live a noble, vital and vigorous life. You will be buffeted in life as in the ocean but will retain control and achieve your goals and dreams. You will come to me as a returning son or daughter.

Your life will flourish as you become aware of your living and eternal spirit.

When your spirit is awakened, it will refresh your life as cool water refreshes thirst. Your well being will be accelerated and flourish. You will become sensitive to the spirits around you. You will be attracted to likeminded individuals without the trial and error of multiple interactions. Their character will be transparent to you during normal and casual meetings. You need not date countless strangers to find the one that you will love. You will be repelled by cold and calculating individuals.

When your eyes are turned inward and veiled, you are aware only of yourself and your own problems. With faith, your eyes are turned out ward, your life is put in perspective and you become sensitive to others.

Your spirit refreshes your life as cool water refreshes your body.

You may ask, if you are part of me, why is it that many of my children appear cruel, selfish and evil. How could it be? It is because with a portion of my spirit you also have free will! You can make your own good and bad decisions!

It is a paradox. If I have given you a portion of my spirit and consciousness then you have the power of creativity and freedom of choice. As a result, a lot of mischief and cruelty is possible. But this does not mean that man is evil and that he is born with sin. No, it only means that man can make bad decisions. As a result, you must learn how to control your power so that you can come back to me pure in spirit.

Your spirit is the central theme of your life. Every action in your life is weighed against your spiritual development. As you recognize your spirit and develop it, your life flourishes. As you ignore it, the fullness of your life diminishes. Your personal development, your interactions with others and your loved ones are reflections and the result of your spiritual behavior.

Every deed and thought of your life impacts upon your spiritual and moral worth. Every aspect of your life is influenced by your moral worth. The development of your moral worth is the reason and purpose of your life. This is the theme and heart of my message to you.

Every deed and thought of your life impacts on your spiritual worth.

You are here to learn how to live without the temptations of greed, jealousy, lust and other vices. Your life is a morality play where all of your actions are evaluated and judged. Do you give fair measure in your business and daily transactions? Do you honor your responsibilities to your family, colleagues and subordinates? Do you honor and value your spouse and treat each other with respect, love and devotion? Do you greet and treat your fellow man with good will?

Your life is a morality play.

As you work out your spiritual life during the day, you continue to resolve daily issues in your dreams and sub consciousness. It is your consciousness freed from your body. Falling asleep is similar to being on the other side. Your dreams think that your waking self is a dream. Time is only a frame work for your growth on earth.

The development of your spirit or moral worth will depend upon hard work and effort on your part. It cannot be vicarious or passive. Faith without practice is empty and without redemption.

Faith without practice is empty and without redemption.

When you finally sojourn with me, you will meet your loved ones who have passed over before you. You will interact with them in renewed relationships when you return to earth. Your rebirth is part of the rhythm of life similar to the trees and flowers as they re-awaken each Spring. Your lives will recycle endlessly until you achieve spiritual perfection.

Chapter 4

Your Spiritual Challenge and Soul

Your Spiritual Challenge
I did not create you to rend the world asunder for your avarice or pride. I did not give you a portion of my spirit without you being responsible for it. You are accountable for its use.

Guilt and remorse are reflections of its abuse. Flesh has no feeling. It is your living spirit that suffers. As a result of sharing a portion of my spirit, your responsibility and power are enormous. Your major challenge, therefore, is to learn how to control your power so that you can come back to me pure in spirit and consumed only by love.

You are accountable for the spirit that I have given to you.

Your spiritual challenge is to grow in spiritual value and moral worth. Your experiences and reactions are a test of your moral worth. Each of you has been given a unique challenge. People and events will come in and out of your life for support or as a challenge to help you to grow and become worthy of returning to my presence. It is your responsibility to grow, develop spiritually and become worthy of the spirit that I have given to you.

Your spiritual journey on earth will not be easy. It will entail many failures and pain. There will be a constant struggle between your best and worst selves. Your happiness and contentment on earth will depend upon your success in this struggle. Otherwise, your well-being and happiness will remain elusive, unless you recognize and persevere in your spiritual challenge.

Your spiritual journey on earth will not be easy.

Your spirit will be challenged and developed over many of your lifetimes. You will be challenged to live in harmony and love with your fellow man and to live without the temptations of greed, jealousy, lust and other vices. You will have many failures and temptations. Indeed, it may take many lifetimes to burn out your imperfections. Events will happen in your life for a reason and it is why there are no coincidences. You are not a random victim. Those with a good heart will remain unharmed or "protected" during their lives. They need not fear the future.

Events happen in your life for a reason and it is why there are no coincidences.

You must endeavor to burn out, control and lose the dross or impurities in your life. It is like burning out the imperfections of gold to bring out its purity. The process is not easy. Every negative act you do will return to you until you learn empathy and gain love. It is not an easy process and may take many lifetimes.

Those of you who do not live in harmony and love with others will face two consequences. The first is that every negative or positive thing that you do to another, you are also doing to yourself. It shapes your character and the future events that will befall you. People like to say, "What goes around comes around". Indeed, this observation is true.

Sooner or later the consequences of your actions will rebound upon you. It is not intended to serve as a punishment but as a means to teach you empathy and how it feels to be treated, hurt or cheated in the same way.

What you do to others you are doing to yourself.

The second consequence is that it will influence your future life. If a man blinds a person in this life, he is destined to be blind in this or the next life. Not as punishment but as atonement, to teach him empathy for the results of his former action. It is not for retribution or revenge but to help that person understand and feel the consequences of his deed.

Do not regret your past failures and actions. You are a different and better person today than you were before. Your spirit has grown as a result of your trials and atonement. Look forward to new trials, opportunities and certain joys to come. You will be a better person in the future as your spiritual journey continues. Your past lives have contributed to your development. Your experiences in this life continue to do so. Do not look back, except to change the thoughts and conditions that may have contributed to your illness and failures.

You will recycle on this earth until you learn to live with grace, love and good will. In essence, you are developing your soul by learning how to control the power of the spirit that I have given to you as it is manifested in your conscious behavior.

You are developing your soul by learning to control the power of my spirit that is in you.

Your Soul

As your spiritual and moral worth grows, your spirit matures and blossoms. The flowering of your spirit represents the maturing of your soul. As a rose bud is to a rose, your spirit is to your soul. Your soul represents the flower of your spirit. It is your awakening spirit.

Without good works and moral worth your spirit is dormant without its flower or soul. As you grow in spiritual worth and control your passions you add to the development of your soul. Your soul is the burning and growing edge of your spirit. It is the heart, the flower and essence of your living and eternal spirit. It is pure love and good will.

Your soul represents the flower of your spirit.

Your spirit grows in purity, from one lifetime to another. As you learn to control your passions and actions, your soul develops. Love flourishes in you as a result of your maturing soul. It is the embodiment of love and good will. As your spiritual self grows in love, you draw closer to me and eventually become one with me in love. At that time, you will be in a total state of bliss and grace. Your spirit and consciousness will exist through eternity in my presence. Your sojourns on earth will have ended and you will no longer need a physical body. You will dwell in my presence forever.

Your soul is the embodiment of love and good will.

Your developed soul is the ultimate result and goal of your journeys on earth. It is that perfect place in you that I wait and long for. It is your return to my being. Your task on earth will have ended. While your body is a vehicle for your spirit, it will no longer be needed in another lifetime on earth.

You can sense your soul in quiet times of contemplation, when you are with your loved ones or surrounded by the beauty of nature. Your soul knows no distance. Whether your loved ones are next door or across the ocean, you can communicate spiritually as if you were together. All souls are as close to each other as if they were in a "tea cup".

All souls are as close to each other as if they were in a "tea cup".

Your spirits can sense each other despite any degree of separation, across the world or across the street. How many times have you thought of a friend when the phone rings? How often do you have the same thoughts as your spouse or friend before they are expressed? You can also sense the presence of your departed ones. Leave your hearts and minds open for this. Lack of belief and faith prevents such communication.

Your spirits can sense each other despite any degree of separation.

A person with an advanced soul shines and emanates love and good will. It is reflected in their eyes and smile. They radiate in the presence of others.

Your soul is not rational. It knows only love.

Chapter 5

Love and Marriage

Love

A pure and loving spirit represents the ultimate goal in the development of your soul. Love is the only reality. Love is that ever present feeling in you that waits to be awakened. It is a yearning and desire that waits to be satisfied. It is your ultimate happiness and fulfillment. When your sojourn on earth is completed you will reside in an aura of love in my presence. Without love, the world would be in chaos and could not exist. Without love, you cannot know me.

Love is the only reality.

Love blossoms forth when two people are attracted to each other. It is an awakening spark between two people when their spirits connect and contribute to each other's spiritual worth and growth. Their interaction accelerates and sustains their spiritual development. Both spirits absorb portions of each other. You love someone who sees and adds value to you.

I love you for seeing the value in me.

The recognition of your spiritual worth and contribution to its growth is the basis of love. It stirs your spirit and accelerates its growth. People of comparable spiritual values generally fall in love with each other. Love is also awakened when a child is born. It is a sacred bonding of the parents and child's spirits. A child picks its parents to renew a spiritual relationship from previous lives or to support its spiritual developmental needs in its new life.

A child picks its parents.

Marriage

While love is pervasive throughout the world between friends and families, its home is in marriage. Those who marry come closer to me and advance their spiritual development. They complete half of their religion. To have one true and enduring love in your life is a precious gift.

Marriage is the home of love.

Marry well. You pick up each other's personalities and spiritual values which become part of you and strengthen you. You accelerate each other's spiritual growth and grow closer to me. To some degree, you meld your spirits. Dwell in love and good will. Do nothing to upset the harmony and peace that you share together. It is a spiritual blessing.

Through love you accelerate each other's spiritual growth and grow closer to me.

Marriage is the center, heart and crucible of your life's interactions. It is a critical test of your spiritual worth. Your spouse is your spiritual partner. Honor and value your spouse and treat each other with respect, love and devotion.

Marriage is the crucible for every good and bad deed between two people. Marriage is not what your spouse owes you or what your spouse can do for you. Marriage is fealty between two people and how they can help each other.

Woe to the person who abuses his or her spouse. They are abusing the spirit of two people, the one abused and themselves. He or she is blessed who is loved or has a loved one.

Your spouse is your spiritual partner.

To marry for any reason less than love is a sin. Your choice of a mate should be compelling. Do not settle or rationalize your choice. If you have to think or rationalize your choice, do not do it. Any reason less than love will end in failure. If a person marries for sex, he or she will find disgust. If they marry only for money, they will earn it as if they had worked for it. If they marry for power or position, they will find emptiness and contempt. The lives of such people will be vainglorious and empty.

Love can generalize to other persons. There are many flowers in my garden that you may be attracted to. Yes, your feelings may weaken and you may be attracted to another, besides your true love. However, maintain your fealty to your spouse. It is yet another moral challenge.

Your choice of a mate should be compelling.

Do not despair for the lack of a loved one or marriage partner. Your loved one waits for you. You will find each other. Have faith and keep a good heart.

Chapter 6

Quality of Life

While your life may be a morality play and a struggle for the development of your spirit, I did not put you on earth to suffer. I want you to be happy and to enjoy the beauty and bounty of the earth. My goal for you is to have the highest quality of life while on earth. I love my creations and I want you to love and enjoy the life that you possess. There is no life without quality of life.

There is no life without quality of life.

Mankind has the capacity for happiness and the enjoyment of all that is beautiful. I have given you the beauty and bounty of the earth for your pleasure and for that of your family and loved ones. This includes your ability to create and enjoy music, art, and fine foods. I have left nothing out for your enjoyment, the pursuit of your dreams and contentment with your achievements. Your creation and life are a gift from me. You are here to live a purposeful positive life. You are in control of your life. It is not random.

Some of you may have guilt about your wealth and success, as compared to those less fortunate. There is no shame in your success or happiness. Take pride in your accomplishments. It does not detract from the life and success of others. It only contributes and helps improve the world and those around you. Live with quality and beauty in your lives. It is a reflection of your spirit and helps to sustain it.

Take Pride in your accomplishments.

I did not put you on earth to suffer or agonize over the misfortune of others. Agonizing over the poor and less fortunate does not help them, except for your charity and manifestations of good will. Your own misfortune would not help them. Your prosperity, however, will help to increase their standard of living and serve as an inspiration for them.

CHAPTER SIX

I love my creations and I want you to prosper.

You are here to develop your loving spirit, to grow, to seek your fulfillment and to enjoy the bounty that I have given to you. As you strive in this respect, I help you in subtle ways. It is your life to enjoy. You create your own happiness by the pursuit of your dreams and beliefs. You create the stress and turmoil in your life because of your negative thoughts and the adverse interactions you have with your fellow beings. You create your own reality with your actions and beliefs.

You create your own reality with your beliefs.

Some of you wait for the return of a deity to create your paradise on earth and to experience rapture. However, your current life on earth is your intended paradise. It is for you to enjoy now, ignore or to destroy. Do not waste the gift and opportunity that I have given to you.

Chapter 7

Power of Belief and Hope

The power of my spirit in you is released through your beliefs and thoughts. Your living and eternal spirit responds to your thoughts and beliefs to create your reality. Your thoughts are "things" in a very literal sense. With your beliefs and thoughts you create your personality, your perceptions and the quality of your life. The power of hypnosis, voodoo, acupuncture and many traditional medicines are due to the power of your spirit that is released through the "power of suggestion". You "hypnotize" yourself every day with your thoughts. On a daily basis, your thoughts act in the same manner as a hyponitst.who uses the power of suggestion to create your reality.

Thoughts are "things".

You achieve your goals and dreams only through your desires, faith and good will. They release the power of your spirit. Unless you set goals for yourself, they cannot materialize. Your deepest desires, however, must be accompanied by faith in their fulfillment. Faith releases the power of your spirit. It transforms the desire into a reality similar to a film negative that creates a positive picture. Without faith your desires cannot materialize from thought to reality.

This process, however, depends upon your good will and good heart. Lack of good will blocks or short circuits the power of your spirit. Without it, both desire and faith cannot function. Thus desire, faith and good will are the magical qualities that focus and accelerate the achievement of your deepest goals.[3] You cannot make promises or bargains with me to achieve your desires.

Your desires will materialize with faith and good will.

You create your own reality with your thoughts and actions. You must dare to dream. But watch what you wish

---

[3] Robert, J, (1994). The Nature of Personal Reality. Novato, Calif: New World Library.

for, your dreams will materialize. You also create many of your own illnesses through your imagination. Often your imagination is influenced by the many medical advertisements that you are exposed to in the media. The power of most medicines, for the same reason, is in the power of suggestion because of your belief in them. Your faith and belief in your own health and well being will help to cure you.

You create your own reality.

I also extend an invisible influence, in addition to the power of your spirit, to shape your life and fulfill your desires. I will aid the worthy in their deepest desires. I will help those who pursue an education or when they buy a house. I intervene to save the worthy from the worst consequences of their own actions or from potential accidents. I frustrate those who abuse their spirits from success in their own desires and enterprises. I also frustrate the worthy, if success will lead to their arrogance and pride. My invisible hand is ever present in your lives.

My invisible hand is ever present in your lives.

The clergy likes to find and promote miracles as a way of proving my existence. Little do they realize that life is the miracle through the power of my spirit that is in you. Your thought, hearing and vision that spring from your flesh are the miracles, not some apparition, illusion or hallucination. You do not need "magic, miracle, and mystery" to prove my existence. You are the proof of my existence.

The miracles that you seek lie in yourself.

Hope

Hope represents your desire to grow, achieve your goals and to succeed. It seeks redemption from your mistakes and failures and the desire to improve. It is the desire for better things to come.

During difficult times, never give up hope of better days. Do not live with regrets for past occurrences. You are no longer the same person. New opportunities and joys wait for you. To say "I can't" in the face of new opportunities is a denial of yourself and your eternal spirit.

Never lose hope for a loved one due to their failures or shortcomings. It dishonors them by not giving them credit to change. It denies them hope. Hope is a form of charity that overlooks their faults and weaknesses. As they face their problems and grow in spiritual value, they become a different person. Give them credit for that and accept it in yourself.

Hope is like faith. It releases the power of your spirit. If you are sick, hope and belief in your recovery will help to assure it. Despair will only help to promote your illness.

Chapter 8

Why Bad Things Happen

You will be challenged by adverse situations on many occasions. You will be severely tried and put under great pressure. Bad things will happen to you. There are multiple reasons for this. Do not despair.

Hardship will occur to test you and to accelerate your growth and spiritual development. Hardship will occur as atonement for your earlier deeds. Hardship will occur when you are being used as a foil to thwart lesser men in their sinful and evil acts. Hardship will occur when you are an innocent victim of someone's malfeasance. Hardship will occur to prevent a greater hardship and misfortune in your future.

You will never understand the reasons for many of these events. My ways are mysterious. However, I never give you

41

adversity greater than you can bear. Persevere, there are immediate and long range reasons for every hardship. Through hardship, you are spiritually transformed into a better and stronger person.

You will have no adversity greater than you can bear.

<u>Hardship as a Challenge.</u>

I will test you through hardship in order for you to learn and bring out your latent capabilities, and to accelerate your spiritual development. It is the better person who is so tested and strengthened for future challenges. Did you fail on a critical task? Did someone falsely accuse you about your professional competence? Did you lose a business opportunity?

Through hardship you are spiritually transformed into a better person.

I give you defeat so that you learn to accept defeat and avoid being vainglorious. I temper you into "steel". Honored is the person who accepts defeat gracefully. While you will regret your loss, you will have other compensating successes the value of which you may underestimate. They will be no less but greater in value.

Misfortune will strengthen your compassion for others. Some seriously disabled individuals overcome crippling limitations and serve as an inspiration to others as they celebrate their own spirit. There is often good in what you otherwise would see as a failure. Have faith. There are reasons for the events in your life that you will eventually understand in this world or the next.

After every difficulty there is relief.

Despite your difficulties, there are kindred spirits who watch over you. They will intervene and come into your life to protect you from undue harm at critical moments of your life. You will be hurt but remain unharmed in the overall scheme of your life. I too intervene to help you in subtle ways. My purpose is to test your mettle as I prepare you for other challenges.

Hardship as Atonement.

Bad things will also happen as a consequence of your former actions. Do those who injure others and steal think that they will not repay or atone for their actions? Whether in this lifetime or the next, they will endure and experience the pain they have inflicted on others, as a means of gaining insight into the consequences of their former behavior.

Eternity is timeless. All of your behaviors will be atoned for until the dross is burned out and it is replaced by empathy and understanding of your former deeds. The process is slow but sure.

I grind very slowly but very finely for your atonement.

Hardship as a Foil.

You may be used to block the adverse actions of others. Human interactions involve the worst and the best characteristics of people. Some of you, however, may be used as foils to thwart the behavior of wrong doers. As a nation must defend itself and change the behavior of aggressors, so must an individual.

I use those close to me as an anvil upon which the offending person will be blocked or broken upon, and as a means to change their behavior. It strengthens my surrogates, although frustrating or painful to them, as they serve my purpose.

People of character and integrity often inspire the resentment of persons of lesser character and presumed self-importance. A person with character reflects the lesser person's imperfections and enhances their insecurity, jealousy and self-doubt. The lesser person will gratuitously try to injure such a person through lies about their character or other means. Some misfortune, however, will find them as a consequence.

Some of you serve as anvils to foil the dishonesty of others.

Yes, good people will suffer loss and hurt, but they will eventually realize that I keep them free of harm in the larger picture. They will eventually witness and wonder at the loss their attackers will inevitably experience. They will begin to wonder what fate other people will have in store for themselves, as a result of their attacks on them.

Hold no animosity. Their hatred will bounce off you and affect only the person who offends. It takes two hands to clap and two people to sustain hatred.

Hardship as an Innocent Victim.

When others assault or defraud you, steal or destroy your property, defend yourself within reason. Do not turn the other cheek. Your acquiescence only emboldens them to further misdeeds. I gave you the means and capability to defend yourselves.

Assure that the offender experiences an equivalent loss.

Your successful counteractions are part of their atonement on my behalf. Wait until the time is right or an opportunity presents itself. Strive to assure that their loss or hurt is equivalent to yours. How else will they learn restraint and cease their behavior? Do not seek revenge only justice. Maintain good will. Do not act with hatred as it will nullify your efforts and injure your own being. Even if you lack the means to seek redress, be patient and maintain good will. You will be surprised by the misfortune that will eventually befall your assailant.

Misfortune will eventually befall your assailant.

Some people act as if there is no tomorrow, as if there is no judgment and that they are immune to the consequences of their actions. They think that when they wake up in the morning, their deeds will not be discovered during the day. Life is full of pitfalls and potential misfortunes which they have unwittingly invited upon themselves.

Your negative thoughts alone will bear upon them. The collective negative thoughts of many people also have a profound effect on the person or persons to which they are directed. You are also my instruments, as foils, for their behavior. Your benign neglect and quiet amusement will also confound them. If you choose, forgiveness is also appropriate. It will be a blessing to you.

Hardship to Prevent a Greater Loss.

Hardship will occur to prevent a greater unknown future loss, or tragedy, that would otherwise befall you. Some prior intervening adverse event could occur to prevent a worse catastrophe in your future. You may have a minor accident in order to avoid a larger tragedy such as a plane crash. The loss of a desired financial transaction could be to prevent an unforeseen bankruptcy in the future. I work in mysterious and unfathomable ways to protect you.

However, unforeseen and tragic an event may be, it is not an entirely random occurrence. What sometimes could be viewed as bad luck, such as having been caught in an earthquake or flood, may be attributable to your attraction to the challenges of that area or scene. Bad luck in business and social situations can also occur due to your actions and inactions. Sometimes good luck will be followed and be balanced by bad luck in order to temper your vain reaction to your good luck.

In a major disaster, when mass and indiscriminate death and loss occur, your living spirit still exists. Although tragic, relative to the larger scheme of your existence, the spirits of the victims continue unabated. The 'just" will rejoice among their formerly departed friends. The "lost" will begin their atonement. All will return to earth until their spiritual journey is completed.

There is no end as there is no beginning to your spiritual journey.

Do not take pleasure in the misfortune of others. You may invite it for yourself. Everyone is tested by their personal trials and misfortunes. You are also tested by your successes.

Chapter 9

Personal Development, Your Body and Health

Personal Development

You were not put on this earth to be a random and aimless creature to be buffeted about and be influenced by forces beyond your control. You are in control of your own life and its outcomes. You are responsible for the development of the capabilities and skills that I have endowed in you. You are here to strive and fulfill your heroic human potential and spiritual development.

You are challenged to evolve from a state of psychological immaturity to the courage of self responsibility, assurance and ultimately, the adventure of being alive. You are on a journey with many trials to overcome. Do you have the courage, the knowledge, the capability to succeed? You will be challenged and become stronger because of it. [4]

You are on a long journey with many trials to overcome.

You honor me and yourself by developing your fullest potential in your career, health and all personal interactions. All capabilities are within you to some degree waiting to be awakened or developed. Develop and exploit what I have given to you. As you do so, only then will I open doors for you and support your success.

Do not sell yourself or your potential short. Do not place "boundaries" on yourself, on what you can or cannot do. Seek the occupation that you desire. Do not limit your desires for presumed lack of support, capability or funds. Pursue your desires. I will help. I rejoice when you fulfill your potential and bring out your greatest potential. Happiness is not wanting or yearning in your own heart, but having strived regardless of outcome and having lived a fulfilling, and accomplished life.

---

4 Campbell, J. (1987). The Power of Myth. New York: Doubleday

A door will open when you strive for your goals.

You will not succeed in every instance and you will make mistakes. You cannot be successful all of the time. Accept your failures. The important thing is to persevere regardless of outcome. Success will eventually follow.

Life is like a "batting average," with some hits and some misses. I expect you to strive and if you fail, try again. Failure is better than no effort at all in trying to achieve your dreams and goals. You will need all of your faculties - mental, emotional, physical and spiritual - to succeed. You will also need the support of your friends and strangers who will come in and out of your life as needed.

Life is like a "batting average" of successes and failures.

Success comes in increments. Do not act in haste. Carefully consider opportunities that come your way, or else, you could repent their loss in leisure. Be patient, persevere and have faith. Your goals are assured. After each success or failure renew and sustain your efforts. To continue your striving is a form of prayer and thanks.

Success comes in increments.

Listen to your intuition. It draws from your eternal spirit and the better spirits who surround you. It represents the accumulated knowledge of your spirit and former experiences. It will try to break through during your times of need, and indeed will alert you in time of danger. To be insensitive to your spirit and intuition is to forfeit your best interests.

Endeavor to get an education and training. They release your potential and will open doors and opportunities for you. It will also expand your mind and enable you to think and become independent from the thoughts and dominance of others. Those who do not exert themselves to become educated, or to gain usable skills, remain pliant and rudderless. They abort their own growth. Their lives will remain shallow and unfulfilled.

Take pride in your job. There is dignity in work and in hard work. Every man takes pleasure in a job well done and in the mastery of their craft. There is also dignity in every person and in their job, no matter how lowly their job may appear to you. Greet every worker with the respect and good will that they deserve. Show your appreciation. By doing so, you also honor yourself. Every job contributes to the needs and fabric of society.

There is dignity in work.

Do not measure yourself by your job, your possessions or your position on the economic ladder. Be proud of who you are as a moral and spiritual person. As you grow in self worth, you will become less aware of yourself and more aware of others. The need for self aggrandizement will decrease. The enhancement of yourself with expensive possessions will no longer be important to you. You will become content in yourself and who you are, without the need to draw attention to yourself. Those who know their worth are no longer self-conscious and their image becomes unimportant. Narcissism is the result of undeveloped personalities and potential.

Be proud of who you are as a moral and spiritual person.

Do not live with fear or anxiety. It will limit your opportunities. You are basically free from harm except for your own behavior and negative thoughts. When you are fearful and afraid of danger, you will attract it to you. Lesser persons with evil intent will be drawn to you and oblige your fears. With belief in your welfare and safety you repel danger and harm. You are not a victim. Only fear the consequences of your own sinful or evil deeds.

Watch your thoughts. If you think you are sickly, or unworthy of success you will create that reality. Do not identify with anything that you do not wish to become. Maintain a positive attitude toward yourself, health and capabilities. To do otherwise can lead to depression. Depression is a spiritual emptiness, a feeling of worthlessness and void in your life. It is also a spiritual yearning for the absence or death of a loved one.

You are free from harm except for your negative thoughts.

As I create, you also create your arts. You create through my creativity, the creativity in your living spirit. Your spirit expresses itself through song, music and art. I enjoy your arts and creativity. When you sing, sing to me. I listen. I enjoy all of your artistic efforts. You create your food recipes, sculptures, your electronic and mechanical inventions and your homes. My creativity resides in you. As you express yourselves, you honor me. Do not hesitate to indulge yourselves in this gift.

When you sing I listen. I enjoy your creative gifts.

I expect you to strive, pursue your dreams and to continually improve yourself. Happiness and contentment are the result of your proactive efforts, sacrifice, and the fulfillment of your desires.

Your Body and Health

Your body is the temple of your spirit on earth. I gave you a perfect body. It is your responsibility to care for it. It has a consciousness of its own and will respond favorably to the least care and exercise that it receives. Do not be slothful and neglect your body's need for nourishing food and exercise. It cannot take care of itself. You will be regretful, if your life is unnecessarily cut short due to lack of care and respect for the beautiful physical instrument that I have given to you.

Your body is the temple of your spirit on earth.

Your body is also affected by your attitudes and beliefs. Your belief in your health or sickness also creates your health or sickness through the power of my spirit in you. Some of you can create unnecessary illnesses, if you feel you are sickly or if you absorb the constant messages of the illnesses promoted in the media. Your beliefs have negative or curative powers. Your positive attitude toward your health, diet and exercise are the best preventative measures.

Your health is affected by your attitudes and beliefs.

Your health is also affected by your personality. Those who live with anger and resentment, subtly stress their bodies with their negative thoughts. Their faces reflect their unhappiness, negativity or defeat.

The good and the bad in your life throw off an aura. A good person's spirit shines through their eyes and face. There are many astute individuals who can read the quality of your life and your character by your facial expression and the aura that you emit.

Do not neglect exercise. Even a small amount goes a long way. Your spirit helps you. It recognizes your desire for an increase in strength and augments the effects of your exercise.

Unless you watch your thoughts, diet, and attitudes and exercise, you will tip your youth and vitality into old age before its time. There are youthful people and old people who are of the same age. Care for your health and watch your thoughts and beliefs about yourself.

No cosmetic or plastic surgery can match the beauty of a person rich in spirit. You cannot disguise your anger, disappointment or the coarse attitudes that are reflected in your face. Your beauty depends upon your health and inner spirit. Any other intervention, such as through cosmetic surgery, will be in vain and transparent.

Chapter 10

Human Relationships, Friends and Happiness

Human Relationships
You are all interconnected by the fabric of your sub-consciousness and spirit. Emotions and feelings flow in a constant undercurrent between you. Your spirits are open to sub-conscious communication. This is why you can anticipate each other's thoughts and can sense the occurrence of some events. You are connected across the street and across the world. All of your spirits can communicate regardless of where you are. Greet each other as spiritual beings. All of your interactions are intertwined and finely balanced at a sub-conscious level.

Your spirits are open to sub-conscious communication.

Your mind, as well as your spirit, is involved when you speak and deal with others. Your thoughts and verbal communication with each other ride on your feelings and emotions. The true intent of your message lies in the emotional undertones of your words. Your good will or hostility is what the other person will sense not the content of your words.

Children learn language in this manner. They associate the words they hear with the meanings that are conveyed by the emotions and intent of their parents. A mother cannot fool her child by her words that are contrary to her emotional intent.

The meaning of your words ride on your emotions.

Do not judge others. Each and every person that you interact with is struggling with their own problems and eternal spirit. Only I know their trials and tribulations and will judge them as they will judge themselves, when they understand the consequences of their behavior. Your perceptions and generalizations can also lead you astray. Do not pre-judge a person based on their background or race. You will deny them the respect that they may deserve.

Do not judge others.

Beware of jealousy. It is a weakness. It can occur when you do not have faith in your own skills or when others gain recognition for skills greater than your own. Do not compare yourselves to others. You do not know what is in their hearts and what burdens they may have. Their burdens may be greater than your own. Jealousy diminishes you and your self worth.

Rejoice in the success of others. Pursue your own skills and have confidence in yourself. Self importance, jealousy or disparagement of the accomplishments of others only detracts from your better self.

Beware of prejudice. Would you enjoy being its recipient? It is the result of a lesser and undiscriminating spirit. It results from the stereotyping of individuals based on the actions of a few. Individuals of advanced development have the insight to evaluate people by who they are rather than by a simple stereotype.

Do not compare yourselves to others.

Be alert to the spiritual development of others. People are at different levels of spiritual development and have invested deeply in their present belief system. Do not challenge their beliefs.

Recognize also the maturity level of the individual that you are dealing with and adapt your speech to their level of understanding. Do not try to reason with a closed mind, walk around them. They are convinced about the certainty of their meager knowledge and prejudice.

Let your behavior and gracious demeanor serve as an example for those who will respond to it. Many will recognize you for who you are and will respond in kind. In times of need and support, they will materialize to aid you. It will include many whom you barely know.

Let your behavior and gracious demeanor serve as an example for others.

Never bend your knee to anyone or be subordinate to them as a fellow human being. You all share the dignity of my spirit.

By catering to others, you do not improve yourself by association with them. Be proud of yourself and your own spiritual worth as a human being. Maintain your love and good will.

You all share the dignity of my spirit.

Do not return anger. Anger can only be sustained if it is reciprocated. I watch over you and will intercede at critical moments.

F riends

People of similar quality attract each other, just as some people can be repelled by others. Pick and cultivate your friends well. You unconsciously pick up some of their characteristics and spiritual values, as an intrinsic part of yourself. Avoid those who are negative in their outlook and without good character. They will pull you down by their attitudes and behavior.

Friends contribute to your spiritual growth or loss. You will meet like-minded friends throughout your life. Honor them and your relationships. Friends will also come in and out of your life, at different times in your life, to help your growth or to aid you in difficult times.

Honor your friends.

Pets are also your friends. They are a part of my consciousness. They share my grace and are part of my spirit. Do not abuse them. Treat all animals with respect, even those that are sacrificed for food or used for burden. They have a limited degree of free will which lacks the challenge of a moral dimension.

Pets know love. They seek quality of life as you do. They reason to some degree. However, their primary reactions are emotional rather than intellectual. They too are your wards as are the children in your care.

Happiness

Happiness is not living in a grand house, or driving an expensive car. Happiness is not moving to and living in a new and exotic land or on a tropical island. It is not having jewels and possessions. It is not being a famous person with the adulation of their admirers. Adulation may fill what otherwise is a void in their lives.

You may ask, why wouldn't people be happy with their possessions and personal recognition? It is because they have the same spiritual development and personality with or without these possessions and recognition. They can be un-fulfilled with a corrosive heart, full of anxiety, ennui and feelings of emptiness relative to their spiritual development.

I do not give you happiness. You earn it through your spiritual striving to fulfill your potential and development of your moral worth. Happiness is the result of striving to meet and achieve your goals. Happiness is having friends, being loved and having a loved one. Happiness is a spirit rich in moral worth. Happiness is dignity, having shouldered and met your responsibilities and earned your own way without abusing others. Happiness is contentment in your inner spirit. It is your reward for being a good and moral person. To live with happiness and a fulfilled life is a blessing.

Happiness is a spirit rich in moral worth.

Chapter 11

Motherhood, Families and Divorce

Motherhood

A mother's love for her child is one of the most pure expressions of love that is closest to my spirit. As parents you are my surrogate! You set the moral example for your children through your behavior, not your words. Through your behavior and treatment of others, they learn their religion. Through your encouragement, your children set their goals and vision for life. They learn their self-worth from your guidance.

Your influence is pervasive. Be aware of the daily role model that you provide for your children. You are the stewards of their growth. You create their reality. The least bit of love that you give to your children blossoms and endures in their hearts forever.

Through a mother's behavior, children learn their religion.

Do not let the pressure of everyday life, and the need to earn a living, detract you from the joys of raising your children. Do not live through your children or use them in order to enhance your own self importance or needs. Be patient when your children cause you problems. They are dealing with their own issues. Their minds will eventually clear and harmony will return. Give them advice and encouragement. They will hear you but may not react. However, your words, or lack thereof, have special meaning for them and will linger in their minds. They will eventually take your advice.

Do not abuse your children. It destroys their spirit and they lose confidence in their own potential. Love, education, moral values and a belief in their own potential are the greatest gifts a parent can give their child. Parents and children remain in each other's hearts forever. The challenge of raising your children is equal to that of developing your own moral worth and spirit. It is also no less a responsibility.

CHAPTER ELEVEN

Parents and children remain in each other's hearts forever.

Before birth, children pick their parents relative to the challenges and the spiritual development that they wish to undertake on earth. There may be any number of reasons for their return and choice of parents. In most cases, it will be with parents of comparable spiritual worth.

Many persons from former lives will return to a family, in order to resolve problems or relationships of a previous lifetime. This can include mothers and fathers who return to become children of their previous children. It can also include friends, former comrades and persons you may have been subordinate to in order to resolve inter-personal conflicts or problems of the past. They return to correct personal failings that delayed their spiritual advancement in the past. Lingering emotions, positive and negative, can be released in the new relationships. Some will return to renew their deep love in a previous life.

Families

As marriage is the crucible of your moral develop-ment, family is the larger context and stage of your spiritual interactions on earth. All of your spiritual weak-nesses and strengths will come into play and be tested. The family is the vehicle for your individual support and growth. It is the place where love can be reinforced or extinguished by your actions. It is the test of your moral worth.

It is also the place where you recover and find peace from your daily pressures. It is your refuge to renew your spirit and love. It is the one place you can be yourself without the control of others. It is your inviolable castle and retreat.

Uncles, brothers, aunts, sisters and grandparents all play a role as support systems. They add to the fabric of your life for the enrichment and growth of your children and yourself.

Your spiritual weaknesses and strengths will come into play and be tested in your family.

Do not break up the unity and harmony of your families. Those who do so because of a flaw in their character such as jealousy, resentment or false pride, commit a grievous act.

They fracture their spirits as they fracture their families. When support is withheld, or the needs of family members are not met, the negative behavior is magnified due to its impact on the larger family. Persevere under such behavior and hope that the spiritual light of the offending person will awaken and apologies are made. Atonement is otherwise long for such individuals.

Those who divide a family commit a lasting sin.

Husbands or wives through their adverse behavior can create a negative influence on their marriage partner. He or she may adopt the same behavior or belief, to their own spiritual loss. Those wives or husbands, who know better but remain silent under the influence of their spouse, share their guilt. A spouse that disrespects the parents or family of their spouse also disrespects their spouse.

Honor your parents. Do not ignore them or your grandparents. He or she who does so will also be neglected by others. They invite unhappiness.

D ivorce

With divorce, life's opportunities are diminished. Life's investments are wasted. It is a failure of maturity and love. It is a failure of spirit. It is partial death in one or both partners and an admission of failure. Do not act in haste. You may repent in leisure. Seek reconciliation, avoid pride and find your former love and dreams. Forgive one another. Root out the reasons. Do not repeat them. Life is change and growth. Keep hope alive. Otherwise, he or she who is at fault will have an unfilled void in their lives. The aggrieved will find happiness again.

When divorced, you may repent in leisure.

For your children, divorce is abandonment. Their parents are sacred to them. The foundation of their lives will be forever disrupted. To look to your needs alone and not theirs is a sin. Grow up. Do not abandon your role as my surrogate to them. The bond of a child to their parents denies death. Even when a parent has died the child feels abandoned.

Chapter 12

Heterosexual and Homosexual Sex

Heterosexual Sex

Sexual desire is the only part of your life where you do not have free will, except in the choice of your partner. I created this irresistible urge to assure the propagation of mankind. Your motivation for procreation is necessary to assure the continuity and purpose of life and your re-occurrence on earth. Without your sexual drive you could not have replenished yourselves after your numerous conflicts, disease and other disasters.

Sex emanates from the body. Love from your spirit. Sex finds its ultimate expression in love. Protect your chastity. Avoid promiscuity. Protect your reputation and your health from disease. Do not sell it for a "cheap coin." Your self control, discrimination and moderation are part of your challenge.

I expect only modesty in men and women. Aside from the differences in sexual organs, men and women are the same, with the same spiritual challenges, emotions and capabilities. Sex related characteristics and stereotypes, however, can be exaggerated and become extreme. Seek moderation in your male and female characteristics and appearance in society.

Sex finds its ultimate expression in love.

I have made men and women attractive and irresistible to each other. Due to the powerful urge of sex, some of you may stray from the bonds of a relationship or marriage. Sexual activity with anyone other than the one you love and have married will spoil, indeed poison your relationship through guilt and loss of trust. While it can affect your relationship, do not let it destroy it. Time will heal your hurt and disappointment. Your love is sacred and should not be undermined.

Homosexuality

Homosexuality is the result of the many forms and permutations of nature that I have created through the variations in your gene structure. Homosexuals do not have a choice about their sexual orientation. Their sex drive is focused on the same rather than the opposite sex. Although it appears unnatural, it is not a sin.

The homosexual person tempers the extreme characteristics of the heterosexual person. However, homosexuals can also go to extremes in their own behavior and stereotypes as they struggle with their conflicting identity.

Generally, the spiritual and physical needs associated with your body develop as male or female `in accordance with your physiology. In some cases, the male or female spirit may seek to experience a relationship with its own sex. This enables the energy of their sex drive to break its boundaries or primary focus on the opposite sex and connect with its own sex. Love also follows in this situation for the same reasons as conventional love.

Do not scorn the homosexual person. It only reveals your own doubt about your own sexuality. You condemn what you fear in yourself. The homosexual person is a member of your human family. Love them as you love yourself. They too are on a voyage of self-discovery, challenge and personal growth.

Chapter 13

Religion, Religious Leaders and Prayer

Religion

I gave you my spirit and you created your religions. Deeply religious people and all men of faith are my children. Regardless of religious affiliation, all faith is the same and all good men of faith are the same and recognize each other.

Man was aware of his spirit and had faith before there was a formal religion. More highly developed individuals sensed me and their eternal spirit. Your faith and spiritual yearning led to your houses of worship.

Many different faiths and paths lead to me. No path is superior to the other. Different religions are only a framework to support your faith. I favor none over the other. I care only for the development of your spirit and moral worth. All good men are of the same religion in their heart and acknowledge each other.

All good men are of the same religion.

The religious impulses that make you a Christian, Jew, Moslem or any other faith are the same. In this regard, you are brothers and should respect each other as brothers. Some claim that a certain prophet is my son. This belief should not detract from your own spiritual divinity. You are all my sons and daughters.

I introduced different religions at different times to suit the nature of the times and people. Unfortunately, it was necessary to send a new messenger from time to time. I did this when your religious leaders introduced distortions to my message; when the message became exclusive; when there was faith without practice; when the message was deified; or when it was captured and used as a vehicle for extremism and control of your lives.

You are all my sons and daughters.

As I refreshed my message, many rushed in to gain ownership with their own interpretations. Unfortunately, your religions have been distorted by zealots who have imposed their own vision. The religious dogmas that are created by them are harmful and unnecessary for your spiritual growth. He who imposes his religion on others is not religious. They who proselytize their religion are in doubt about it. They need converts in order to reassure and convince themselves about the validity of their own beliefs.

Your purpose on earth is to develop your moral worth and eventually dwell with me in love and peace. Your religions are only a path, a guide, on this quest. A person does not have to be religious to have an ethical code. Many good hearts find me. Many paths lead to me. Poverty and denial are not a prerequisite for faith nor is prosperity the antithesis of faith.

Many paths lead to me.

Religious Leaders
There are many fine religious leaders of all religious persuasions who speak in my name. They awaken the spirit in your heart and help you in your spiritual

development and comfort you in your time of need. They help you grieve and support the important periods and transitions of your life, such as birth, marriage or the death of a loved one. They serve as my shepherds. You will know them by their open and sweet spirit and the temperance of their words. All religious organizations are a blessing for their work in social and community affairs.

It is also an unfortunate paradox that some of those who presume to serve as religious leaders are often the most wicked and flawed among you. They swallow a "book" and fail to understand the elemental and essential truth of my message. They use my mantle as a means to glorify themselves and to dignify what otherwise cannot be dignified in their behavior.

Beware of these so called religious people or "false prophets" who preach words without understanding, and spread malicious dogma for their own needs, self importance and your domination. They repeat empty dogmas and do not provide spiritual guidance for your everyday problems and challenges. They fail to communicate my message. They are my uninvited spokesmen and are not necessary for your spiritual development. They are the antithesis of my message to you.

Be alert to the false witness with words devoid of love and understanding. Beware of those with extreme dogmas that are contrary to the spirit in your heart. Beware of those who speak pious words with a malicious heart. They mock me with their dogmas and empty rituals.

Religious leaders, who denigrate other religions to enhance their own religion, shame themselves. The denigration of other religions does not enhance the truth of their religion. Their words lead to intolerance and war. Such leaders will be unwelcome at my side, until they have learned the enormity of their distortions and misdeeds. Only faith, love and good will should be their message.

The denigration of other religions does not enhance the truth of one's own religion.

Multiple religions and voices, let alone the voice of one man at the apex of a major religion, can scarcely capture the intent and implied meaning of my message. A diversity of interpretation helps to provide some safeguards against the distortions and extreme views that are propagated in my name.

Extremist religious leaders are fanatics. They justify and rationalize their attacks on others in the name of religion. They use my name in vain with their distorted dogmas and beliefs. The zealots of every religion are the same. It matters not which religion they presume to speak for. They are not men of faith. They poison relationships with other religions and groups. Good will suffers in their presence. Those who kill in the name of religion are lost souls, despicable and deranged.

Every good man who lives an exemplary life is a religious leader through their example.

The leaders of some religious cults boast of being former sinners. Their new profession of faith merely masks their sins. Sins cannot be atoned for in a sudden revelation or conversion. The aspects of your character and moral worth must be proven and developed over time with dedication. There is no spiritual gain without good works or atonement for former sins. It is a good man who is led to become a religious leader and not a suddenly reformed sinner who seeks fame, recognition and financial gain.

It is enough for people to follow the faith or spiritual yearning in their own heart.

Religious leaders should serve as teachers without compulsion or coercion. They should assist people in their religious growth. They should speak with moderation and not propagate or market extreme views. Every good man who lives an exemplary life is a religious leader through his example.

It is enough for people to follow the faith or yearning in their own heart. To the extent possible, each person should interpret their particular religion and its writings by their own efforts and understanding. Follow only your own spiritual insights and feelings. Question any dogmas that require you to suspend your disbelief. Question any beliefs that go against your instincts. Listen to that quiet voice in your spirit and your intuitions when your heart resists the assertions of the self serving.

Beware of those who speak pious words with a malicious heart.

Prayer

You pray to me and I listen. Through your prayers, you also release the power of your living and eternal spirit that resides in you. As a result, your prayer is also its own answer. Your prayers reach me through our shared spirit. They do not go to other Gods or intermediaries. The effectiveness of your prayers depends upon a good heart and your good deeds. They are thwarted by the self serving and malicious heart. Your good deeds are also a form of prayer.

Prayer is its own answer.

My people prayed to me in their quiet moments, before there were formal religions. In addition to your great cathedrals and places of worship, let the beauty of the world around you, such as the forest, the meadow and the seaside serve as your cathedral. Pray to me from wherever you may be, when you are moved by my spirit or need me. Your prayers reach me from every location. I hear your many prayers, the way you hear a great chorus. "God willing" is not an empty phrase.

"God willing" is not an empty phrase.

Pray to me but do not worship me or devote yourselves to me. Serve others. Focus only on the development of your own spirit and spiritual responsibilities. Do not confess your sins but atone for them. I benefit not from your confession. It would be far better if you confessed your good deeds. Rejoice in your good deeds. Your fasts, penances and abstinence do not reach me. While they will help to strength your discipline, only your love, good will and charity reach me. No one is born in sin and you do not need an intermediary to atone or to reach me. Only you can atone for your sins.

Confess and rejoice in your good deeds.

As you pray to me, I pray for you. What are my prayers or wishes for you? They are simply that you are worthy of the life that I have given to you, that you strive to meet the challenges that I have set for you, and that you walk in my path of love, good will and charity.

Chapter 14

A Good Person

Your spiritual goal is to become a good person. A good person is not defined by their level of educational achievement, income level, job prestige or social standing. They are defined by their moral structure. They can be recognized by their modesty, perseverance in hardship, their discipline under stress, their courage to take risks, to do their duty and to take care of their families. They are also candid, sincere, know who they are and have quiet self-esteem. Many "respected' persons in society fall short of these criteria.

A good person is known by their moral rather than their social stature.

Today the spirit can be overwhelmed and drowned out by the incessant drum beat of the media and its rush to the lowest common denominator. The rules of decorum, polite conversation and courtship are lost. Sex and indecency are exploited by the media. In such an environment, many lose their way. You must not succumb. Listen to that small voice of your spirit that will not be extinguished. Resist temptation and do not commit moral suicide. Love, decency, and virtue are real. They will follow and grow.

Love, decency and virtue are real.

A good person is the epitome of goodwill. They are known by their treatment of others. They do not intentionally hurt anyone with a harsh word or rudeness. They do not exploit or use anyone for their personal gain. They are considerate, loyal and greet others with good will. They help the less fortunate and help others grow and prosper. They honor their contracts and keep their word and do not abuse their position or authority. They give each person their due and do not cater to garner favor. Their heart harbors no animosity. They come to the support of others when injustice is done, and defend them against injustice. They visit the sick and give words of encouragement to the despondent. They do not judge lest they be judged.

They are generous in their charity. They go beyond writing checks to worthy organizations and recognize the need of those around them. They overlook the frailties of older people, are patient with hyperactive children and rude individuals. They help those in need when not asked, speak well of others who have been maligned and support the advancement of their friends and colleagues. They are a dissenting voice against injustice.

A good person is a dissecting voice against injustice.

They have a fierce moral clarity. They do not compromise their standards to please others. They challenge the malicious gossip of others and do not join in less than honorable deeds. They are known by their personal behavior and the indivisibility of their integrity. They are modest, neither loud nor brash, without excessive display of wealth or position. They are not haughty, prideful or vainglorious. They are patient in adversity and do not complain in hardship. They exhibit a quiet moral courage.

A good person has a fierce moral clarity and courage.

The influence of a good person is beyond calculation. Whether they live in a humble home or in a mansion, they have a great impact on the world. They, unknowingly, influence the spirits and well-being of people far and near. Their words of encouragement, or good deeds, are repeated by those they have touched. They reinforce and support others with their smiles, love and warmth. They serve as a model for others. Like stone hitting water, their impact ripples endlessly to support and sustain others.

The influence of a good person is beyond calculation.

A good person helps to stabilize the world and assure its orderly functioning. The integrity of a good person is the foundation of commerce and contributes to the safety of society. A good person is the quiet basis of peace and prosperity and is the counterweight to those who use and abuse the world and its people for their own gain. You only have to look at peaceful societies and those that are torn asunder, to understand what occurs when there is a deficit of good people. I wait for such a person. They shall be honored in my presence. They are one with me.

The deeds of a good person ripples outwards, like stone hitting water.

Because of their sweet and unassuming spirit they are unaware of their influence, and wonder what they have contributed to the world. Their ultimate success in life is not having hurt any person by word, deed or act and not owing any person an apology for wrong doing or injury. When they pass over, they come to me "clean" and as an unencumbered spirit.

Your ultimate success is not having hurt anyone.

By contrast, the arrogance of the rude and self-serving person hangs like a "cloud" over all those they associate with. Their presence is an offense to many. They are a plague to themselves and others. They find no joy or contentment in their possessions and live with a contentious heart. Their spirits are hollow and vacuous. Many display wealth or use their position to enhance their self importance. However, they have diminished stature among people and receive no respect from them or enjoy any self satisfaction.

You may live or work among the self-serving and deceitful persons. Your spirit may figuratively sense the "stench" of a barnyard among them. "Hold" your nose in their presence. Show forbearance, do not support or give approbation to their behavior.

A good person has an indivisible integrity.

It is possible for you to remain a good person. It is possible to be a good neighbor and to live a good life. Truth and beauty exist. A good person is far happier than those who proclaim their self-importance and wealth. Being a good person is your "badge of honor" and success.

Everything good that you do becomes a part of you.

Chapter 15

Sin and Evil

Sin

You were not born in sin. Each newborn is a fresh spirit of unabated love and expectation. You sin when you do things unworthy of yourself and when its consequences have an impact on others. You sin when you fall short of your ideals and succumb to your weaknesses. You sin when you are self-centered and self-serving, and think only of yourself. You sin when you abuse your position of responsibility and trust. Sin detracts from your spiritual worth and development.

It is a sin:

- To be arrogant and vain. It reveals a vacuous, self-centered person without warmth.

- To insult and disparage another. It is a direct affront to your own spirit.

- To return a gift or a hand of friendship when offered. It is the denial of good will and reveals a malicious heart.

- To remain silent during an injustice. It is to share in the injustice.

- To abuse or hurt a child. It destroys their confidence and inhibits their spiritual growth.

-To fail to report criminal activity to authorities on the false premise of having a "code of honor." It is to condone the activity.

-To take advantage of your subordinates and clients. It is a betrayal of trust.

-To steal, give short measure, or act recklessly. It is a lack of concern for others.

-To have excessive pride. It can diminish an otherwise fine spirit. It will lead to failure of one's plans, until their pride is lost.

He who remains silent during an injustice shares in it.

When you go out of our way to hurt someone, you invite misfortune to follow you. Through your sins you cut off part of my spirit in yourself and reduce your moral worth. What you have done to others will eventually be done to you in this or other lifetimes, until you have understood the impact of your actions, learned empathy and atoned for your actions.

What you do to others, you are doing to yourself.

All sins go to the same place. They lead to the loss of your moral worth. You invite your own atonement. It will surely follow in both miniscule and major ways. As your moral worth decreases, your life becomes more turbulent and capricious and at the mercy of negative influences. As your moral worth increases, your life becomes more secure and follows your dreams. Your atonement is balanced on "a knife's edge."

Your atonement is finely balanced on "a knife's edge."

At birth you are a creature of sweet innocence with a new and fresh challenge to develop your spiritual worth. Do not lose that sweet spirit through sinful acts. Do not let it slip away and become a hard and cynical person. You are here to work out past imperfections. Do not add to them.

Your less than desirable characteristics are transparent to many. They will avoid you in their daily dealings. You fool only yourself with your guile and you will be played the fool sooner or later. Ill gotten gains come with a corrosive heart. Those who defraud their customers also undermine their commercial viability and begin their eventual business decline.

Do not let that sweet spirit of your childhood slip away into a cynical and hard person.

Evil
There is no devil or evil presence in the world in opposition to my "Law of Love". However, there are evil acts deliberately committed against others due to false perceptions and the emotional arousal of less spiritually developed people. Free will enables people to act out their most noble or vile impulses. The behavior of some individuals, as a result, lacks moral restraint.

There is no devil or evil presence in the world in opposition to my "Law of Love".

Evil occurs when there is a false perception of some assumed greater good, worthy cause or for revenge. They rationalize their behavior on their distorted beliefs. Love becomes extinguished in their hearts. Their hatred is aroused and runs unabated and feeds upon its self. They engage in a self-reinforcing cycle of anti-social behavior. They undermine the fabric of society. They fail to understand the impact of their actions on their victims and themselves.

Evil occurs for the pleasure, self satisfaction or gain that it brings to the perpetrator. They think that they are enhancing themselves or demonstrating their power. They are, however, only quelling their innate inferiority and hatred, whose fires will only extinguish slowly.

There is no evil or devil, only evil deeds of misguided or morally less developed people.

To take another person's life is the greatest evil. Those who take the life of another have also offended me. I am a part of each of you. A part of my spirit is also lost. Only I and the person's spirit can make that decision. I gave life and it is for me and the person involved to decide when to relinquish it.

No man has the spiritual right to judge when another person should die. Juries and judges do not have the moral insight to judge a person. Their own moral structure may be lacking and may be unable to judge fairly. Too often juries and judges condemn the wrong person. The decision to condemn a person to death will linger in their hearts and shorten their own lives.

Let a murderer repent in leisure about their evil deed. They have made their bed and created their own "hell." No censure or punishment that you can administer will be greater than the self-punishment that the evil doer will experience in their own minds as a result of their deeds.

Other evils include:
-To falsely imprison or deny someone their freedom. Prosecutors who knowingly convict innocent people will have a comparable debt to pay.

-To prescribe unnecessary, and possibly dangerous, medical treatments for personal gain. Physicians, who do so, betraying the trust of their patients, are like animals of prey.

-To bear false witness, falsely slander a virtuous person or to denigrate a person's character for personal gain.

-To physically abuse the defenseless and force people into degrading acts such as prostitution.

-To deny someone an opportunity that they have rightfully earned for religious, racial or other reason.

To abuse the trust associated with your position is a shameful betrayal.

There are also abominations or greater evils. These are rulers who murder their people, leaders who undermine their democracies for increased power, tyrants who reduce their populations to poverty for personal gain, and totalitarian despots who destroy their own and other nations through war. It includes nationalistic bigots who seek power over their immediate neighbors, and religious fanatics who use religion to impose their perverse dogmas or sexual perversions on their followers. Such events have occurred in the recent past and continue in some form today. The perpetrators have a special atonement waiting for them.

Your character is your destiny.

The evil person lacks empathy and does not feel the pain of others. Their spirit is dormant and their soul lies fallow. There is accountability for all evil and sinful deeds. People may think that they are unobserved and will not be detected. They may think that they are untouchable or immune to consequences. They may leave home in the morning smug in the thought that their fraudulent behavior will not be found out. They are often deranged and cannot quench the fires in their spirit. Their evil acts are a form of 'self-exorcism' of the hatred in their own hearts. The smallest of their deeds are observed and transparent to the spirit world and to others around them.

The smallest of evil deeds are observed and transparent to the spirit world.

They only deceive and diminish themselves. Despite their guile, self-satisfaction and feelings of invincibility, the evil doers will suffer in their lives and spirits far more than the suffering that they may inflict upon others. They incur a heavy debt on their souls and will be challenged severely in many lifetimes. What they think is a solid foundation in their lives is "shifting sand". Their lives will be fragile and can become unraveled at any moment. Anything can happen at any time and will be to their immediate or future loss whether in health, position or family. They shall be deemed among the lost and shall atone in "spiritual darkness" for centuries, until the enormity of their deeds are realized and atoned for. The consequences of their actions will eventually become clear to them. Their atonement and retribution are sure and ordained.

Nations also suffer consequences for the adverse actions of their leaders and followers, through natural, economic and other means.

Sinful and evil persons only deceive and diminish themselves.

Resist your lesser self; do not diminish your spirit. Come back to me. I wait for you. Do not sin and commit shameful deeds. Come back to me and accept my love.

Come back to me. I wait for you.

Those of you who strive to increase your spiritual worth are free of harm. If you are a victim, return an adverse act in a comparable way, when possible. You are also an instrument of my atonement. The perpetrators must understand the consequences of their actions, in order for them to stop. Your forgiveness of them will be a blessing to you, but it will not mitigate their atonement. When someone does a good deed for you, double and return their gesture.

Double every good deed that you receive.

Chapter 16

Age and Death

Age

If you feel that you are only flesh and a victim of age, so shall it be. Your body will deteriorate in accordance with your beliefs. Your older age is not the end but the threshold of a new beginning. While your body ages, your spirit grows.

Your spirit is ageless and forever young. It changes and grows in its moral worth as you progress on your spiritual journey. Only your physical body gets older. You feel only the spirit within you and not your physical age. It is why you do not readily identify with the person that you see in the mirror when you are older. In the eyes of your loved one, you never age.

Many of you age yourselves prematurely and unnecessarily. You age by abusing the beautiful body that I have given to you. You age because of drugs, excessive alcohol and tobacco. You age because of over indulgence in your diet and for lack of exercise. These behaviors can be considered a sin against yourself, since you reduce the quality of your life and shorten your spiritual development.

Your spirit is ageless and eternally young.

Your physical age is further affected by your attitudes, perceptions and expectations. You age because you think you are supposed to age. You age by watching and emulating others as they age. You age by adopting your "image" of old age. You age in the same manner that you pick up local accents and by adopting local expectations and perceptions. Some people unconsciously model themselves after the older people that they see or associate with in their area. Ultimately, your true age is your attitude toward age.

Your true age is your attitude toward age.

As you mature, do not stop your plans or dreams. Your future is ever young with opportunity. While earlier goals may have been met, make new plans and strive toward them. You are younger than you think and your potential for growth remains. By planning, your plans pull you into the future. Not to continue planning and striving as you grow older, will only hasten your decline.

Your plans pull you into the future.

Do not assume an attitude of defeat and hopelessness and wait for your demise, as some older people do. Do not enter assisted living or nursing homes unless absolutely necessary. It is a voluntary acceptance of your demise and will accelerate it. Grow older with grace and maturity and live your life to the fullest to the last moment. As a rose grows in maturity, through its various phases, so should you endeavor in your life time.

Do not dwell on sickness and nurse your illnesses.

Those fortunate to have grown with spiritual beauty, retain that beauty and age with grace. Some individuals fail to grow in spiritual worth and beauty. They fail to become a warm and loving "human being" despite their age. It reflects in their appearance and behavior. They continue and persist in their angry and unhappy ways.

Those who age with grace, pass over with grace. Those who do not age with grace, pass over with resistance and hardship. Your time on earth is finite. Do not squander it. What you may lose in physical decline, you gain in wisdom, insight and maturity.

Those who age with grace, pass over with grace.

As you age, do not despair that your life is almost over. It is ever expanding with new life and adventures to come whether on my side or on earth again. Pass over with youthful anticipation. Do not hold on to a concept of decay and death.

Death
When you pass over, you will fly to me as a bird flies to its nest. As birth is the morning of a new day, death is only the evening. Death is merely a change of

form whereby your consciousness departs and continues without your body. Your consciousness continues in my presence. Your death is part of another cycle, the price of birth, to consolidate your worldly experiences. You will review your experiences on earth, to determine if your goals have been met. You will meet your loved ones who have gone on before. They wait for you. Parents will rush to meet their children. Your friends will once again embrace you.

When you pass over, you will fly to me as a bird flies to its nest.

Do not fear death, but only fear the person you are at the time of death. Those who bring an open and wholesome heart will rejoice and continue their growth in their new dimension. Those who have inflicted harm and hatred will dwell in their deeds and repent of them until that time they can return to earth to make amends.

Do not fear death, but only fear the person you are at the time of death.

All souls will come to me bare and exposed. There will be no deception or false pride. The richest and most powerful will be equal to the simplest man. He who comes to me with a pure and open heart shall be honored. The richest and most powerful of men with shameful deeds will be considered among the lowest. A person's celebrity status on earth, depending on how it was earned, can become a badge of shame.

He who has done no harm to others will be closest to me

What do I want from you when you die? I don't want your riches, jewels or homes. I am not interested in your titles and worldly accomplishments. I only want to know your good deeds. Did you leave the world a better place than you found it? Did you help your fellow man when his need was obvious and without being asked? Did you add to the paradise that I created for you? Did you leave without debt or harm to any one? Strive to die rich in the good deeds, memory and love that you leave behind.

When you die, you are taking another trip. Your luggage, however, is the sum and balance of your good and evil deeds. During your lifetime, you are in the process of packing for your trip to my side. You bring only your living and eternal spirit and the negative and positive aspects of your behavior on earth. Just as you look forward to any trip, have the same anticipation for your sojourn with me. If you bring luggage full of evil deeds, such as deceit and harm to others, you will dwell in remorse about them. If your luggage is full of beauty, happiness and good deeds they will be reflected in your new home and carried over to your next life on earth.

When you pass over, you are taking another journey. Your luggage is the sum of your good and bad deeds.

You unconsciously choose the time of your death, when your spiritual task is completed. In some cases, it is preordained depending upon your spiritual goals. It will occur when your immediate spiritual mission has been fulfilled, when you wish to join your loved ones who have gone on before you, or when your spiritual growth has reached a temporary stopping point and needs consolidation. You may also die young as atonement for former deeds.

Your graveyards are places of deception. Only that which has belonged to the earth has returned to it. Your graveyards support the illusions of those who believe that there is only one life. Treat the grave site as a memorial to your loved one's living and eternal spirit. What lies there belongs only to the earth. Their spirit and reality is with me. Go to the resting place of their remains only to help bring their memory and spirit closer to you. To consider them dead is to deny their living spirit. It is your spirit that sheds it's body, not your body that gives up its spirit! They are only dead who are dead in spirit.

They are only dead who are dead in spirit.

Chapter 17

Grief and Despair

Grief

Grieve for your friends and family who pass over. Pray that their spirits have an easy transition. Remember that only the body of your loved one has died. Grieve only for their temporary loss to you. Their spirit lives and is near you. Think of them and draw them near to you. Your love and thoughts will help them in their passage and keep them near you. Remember also that one day you will again see their easy smiles and greet their warm hearts.

It is your spirit that sheds its body, not your body that gives up its spirit!

They will wait for you and in some cases are close to you, at this very moment. Love is forever and hovers around the loved one and those who yearn for their loved ones. When your loved one leaves in the morning, his or her memory remains fresh in your mind until they return at night. It should be the same with the memory of your departed loved one, until you meet again. Keep their memory fresh. Their consciousness exists and is near you. You will be reunited again. One day is as a thousand years and a thousand years is but one day.

The spirits of those who have passed over hover around you.

When your departed loved ones realize that they still exist, your belief in the finality of death frustrate their efforts to reach you. Do not think of your departed as dead, it puts a veil between you. It blocks their thoughts and spirit. Do not deny and abandon the reality of their living and eternal spirit. It denies you the reality of their memory and existence.

CHAPTER NINETEEN

Think of your lost loved ones and draw them close to you.

Despair
Throughout your life, you will have many disappointments. They will happen periodically. They will not be more than you can bear with certain relief to follow. In many cases, you will be consumed by pain and sorrow. Do not despair. I know and share your pain and hold it as my own.

Reflect and learn from the reasons that may have led to your despair. Know that it is an integral part of your spiritual development and understanding. Perhaps some degree of atonement may be involved. Whatever reason, they are for your personal growth, development and compassion for others. Have faith. Be patient, the reasons for your despair will be resolved and overcome in due time.

No one is an "island" or independent of my love and judgment. Your spiritual development is the goal of your life, whether you realize it or not. If all of the pain in your life was concentrated into one day, you could not survive it. Similarly, if all of your happiness was concentrated into one day you could not survive it. Your growth and development, pain and happiness, comes in incremental phases for your personal challenge and spiritual development.

When in despair, you may cry out why? For those who believe in me, you may ask what do you want from me? I want your spiritual growth. I want your love for others to blossom. I want you to become a role model for others as a good person. I want you to appreciate the gift of life that I have given to you. I want you to develop the capabilities that I have instilled in you. I want your success and happiness. I want you to come back to me with an open and pure heart. Your grief and pain is but one step in this goal.

Chapter 18

Suicide, Abortion, and Adoption

Suicide

Life is precious. Suicide is the denial of my gift of life. Those who commit suicide fail to meet their allotted challenge in life. They will dwell in a state of regret in my presence until they return to face the problems that they had avoided. It is a lack of hope and a lack of faith that events cannot change to their advantage. Suicide interrupts your spiritual development. You falsely pre-judge your future and miss unknown joys and opportunities.

Life is a precious gift.

Self-pity, punishment of another, sacrifice for others are not an excuse to end your life. A multitude of other people would trade their problems for yours. Have the courage of life. Do not deceive yourself by temporary and passing problems.

Have the courage of life.

It is a selfish act to those you have left behind. It deprives them of your love and support. It accomplishes nothing and punishes your loved ones. Do not voluntarily return my gift of life to you. You will learn to regret it as you understand the import of your action and atone for it in the hereafter and during other lifetimes.

Do not return your life to me voluntarily.

Those who put conditions on life, that are not met, are prone to suicide. They must realize that their goals will not be met on their schedule or time table. Their desires will work out in due time, on a schedule unknown to them. Only you can propose but I dispose.

Do not put conditions on life.

Those who take their own lives will dwell in the regret of their decision until they return to earth to make amends to those they have affected. They shall face new and harder challenges to compensate and atone for their former action. They may lose their life unwillingly at an early age, to understand the value of the gift they had formerly and willingly forfeited.

Do not despair. I provide. I give each of you only burdens that you can bear. There is relief after every difficulty. Do not disappoint me. Persevere in your goals and the challenges that I have set for you.

After every difficulty there is relief.

Abortion

My spirit enters a fetus in the womb when its heart starts to beat. Until then, the fetus is part of the mother's flesh. The abortion of a fetus with a beating heart, when my spirit has entered, deprives a new spirit of their life. The mother's life will be shrouded in grief for her deed and loss. Her act will linger in her heart.

My spirit enters a fetus with a beating heart.

There is no shame in having a child. It is a blessing to you. Do not prejudge your future. I will provide. Many doors will open. Many good families also wait for children to adopt. Have faith. I am with you.

Adoption
You are more than your genes. While you are close to your biological parents in your gene structure, you may not be as close in your spiritual development. The child's spiritual needs for continued growth may be at variance with the spiritual development of their parents. For this reason, birth through conception can be as random spiritually as birth through adoption.

Adoptive parents are also my surrogates. Their love and devotion, or lack thereof, does not differ from that that of biological parents. It is a blessing for those who adopt. Although the child will someday seek its biological connections, they will understand that the love of their adoptive parents is no less genuine.

Chapter 19

Heaven, Hell and Reincarnation

Heaven

After you pass over and have adjusted to the loss of your body, the degree of your spiritual adjustment will be relative to the state of your spirit at the time of passing. If you have denied me, then you will reside with me in confusion. It you have committed evil you will reside with me in darkness. Your spiritual state and continued growth will depend upon its level of development at the time of your death.

Those who have proven themselves and have added to their spiritual development will dwell in my presence and continue their mental and spiritual growth in what you call heaven. They will be in a state of consciousness devoid of their body.

Falling asleep and dreaming are similar to passing to the other side. In heaven, you will view your earthly life as a dream. You will continue to resolve issues and consolidate the experiences of your past life.

You will view your earthly life as a dream.

You will travel within my greater spiritual universe and contemplate your former lives and experiences. Loved ones will greet you. They are waiting and know when you pass over. A parent's excitement on this side is a joy to behold as they greet their children. You will be reunited in love. You will revive social relationships and rejoice in the love and friends around you. This will be your heaven, the heaven that you have created with the deeds and spiritual growth of your life on earth.

Every mother and father in heaven knows when their child passes over.

Hell

Those who have sinned excessively and committed evil deeds will find themselves in a state of "hell." There is no physical place of hell. They will still be in my presence but they will be in a spiritual state of what they perceive as "hell", relative to the degree of their deeds and moral worth. It will begin at the moment of their passing as they sense that there is no one to grieve for them. Their hell, their atonement and contemplation of their former sins, will begin at that very moment in the thoughts of those they have injured and offended.

Those who have committed evil acts and the worst among you will go into a nightmare like slumber of tortured thoughts. It will be their "dark night." They will be aware of me but feel abandoned by me. Their feelings and emotions will be similar to those they have experienced on earth such as guilt, remorse, regret and shame. This will be their hell. It will continue until they gain some insight into their behavior and are ready to return to life on earth.

Hell is a dark night of remorse.

Hell is not a place of fire and brimstone but a place of darkness, disturbing dreams and thoughts devoid of love. There is no other hell. I do not punish you. You punish yourself with the deeds you have committed on earth and the bed that you have made for yourself while on earth.

Your heaven and hell is also influenced by the memory that people on earth retain of you. Those in hell, their spiritual hell, will suffer from the negative thoughts of those who remain on earth. The negative thoughts of the living will still reach them and leave them no peace until their atonement. Those with good deeds shall dwell in bliss, in the thoughts of their loved ones and will be close to me. Are you held in contempt or love? These feelings and attitudes about your memory will reach you and add to your pleasure or discomfort in my presence.

Your hell will be shrouded by people's memory of you.

Reincarnation
Like nature you have your seasons and cycles. You will be reborn as sure as the sun rises each morning. You will return like the leaves in the Spring, as

Spring follows Winter. As a tree becomes dormant and grows in strength with each Winter season, so does your spiritual strength mature. Each rebirth renews and refreshes the world with new energy and with former mental boundaries and constraints erased. The signs of rebirth are all around you. The flower returns from the seed or bulb. It is not the same identical flower but it springs from its original being or source.

You will be reborn as sure as the sun rises each morning.

During your sojourn with me, your experiences in former lives will have been mulled over and insights consolidated. You will bring back to earth the level of your previous spirit as formerly developed on earth and as refined and matured in my presence. You will continue your spiritual development at a more advanced stage and help others in their growth. Some may still continue to suffer in order to complete their atonement or to fully assure their repentance and empathy. You do not return as a blank page.

The sophistication and emotional maturity of some people are a carryover of their previous lives and development. Notice the sociability and personality of small children. It could not be developed in their short lives. It is the result and testament of their earlier sojourn on earth which has been brought forward.

You do not return as a blank page.

Some of you have spirits older than others and are more sensitive for the love and responsibility to your fellow man. Some, whose lives had been cut off early, will return to visit loved ones or children who they had not had a chance to know in their previous life. The thoughts and prayers of their loved ones will also help to bring them back.

The sweetness and maturity of small children is a testament of their previous lives.

Your re-birth is a new beginning and fresh challenge for you without the burden of false beliefs and old regrets. As you mature, you are once again faced with possible misdeeds, disappointments and regrets. However, each day is a new beginning for your spirit. Your spiritual growth and development will continue as other facets of your eternal spirit are challenged. Your new life will either blossom or face severe challenges depending upon your moral worth or debt.

Chapter 20

Racial and National Diversity

Racial Diversity

Why are there different races? Like flowers I created different colors in man that approach the spectrum of the rainbow, so that you could recognize each other and be different from each other. I created diversity among people to challenge your personal growth through interaction with one another.

Each race excels in some characteristics, but shares in them all. Together you are my garden of colors and capabilities. It is part of my creativity expressed through diversity. Through your differences and interactions, you accelerate each other's development and gain from each other's practices and culture. Together you are a perfect whole.

The sum of all races is a perfect whole.

One race or culture is not superior to another in terms of spiritual value and quality of life. Some industrial nations think that they are superior because of their material development and, as a result, think that they have a right to exploit or dominate others. One cannot assume that one culture is superior to another, when it is the development of the soul and not the acquisition of material possessions that is important.

Some races may appear culturally and materially inferior to you, yet their spiritual worth is equal to any other and they face the same spiritual challenge. The humanity of man is a constant regardless of culture, and can be found in the most remote corner of the world. The richest nations can have a poverty of spirit.

The humanity of man is a constant regardless of race or culture.

Similar races are prone to conflict due to the rejection of what they see of themselves in the other. This in part explains the persecution of one similar group by another, as witnessed in recent history in Europe and the Middle East. They are closer in their characteristics than they realize. Strife due to racial, religious or cultural differences is also due to less developed souls who hate themselves.

Individuals of some races think that they are superior to others and that others, unlike themselves, are less human and less important. Such people pay a price for their attitudes and behavior through defeat or persecution. Some racial groups were dispersed by me in the ancient past. If they had remained as a united national group, they would have brought grief to their neighbors. All races must tolerate the differences between them and not subjugate those they think are inferior people.

Strife due to racial, religious or cultural differences is due to less developed souls who hate themselves.

National Diversity
As the personalities of people differ, so do the personal characteristics of people of different nations. The variations of the personalities of different nations

also represent different parts of a perfect whole. Nations interact and balance each other much like the interactions of individual people. They are a part of my larger plan to create checks and balances between the different agendas and personalities of various nations.

The national origins of its citizens explain the success of America. America, as a new nation, lacks the restrictive attitudes and restrictions of older societies. As a result, its potential is unleashed. In America, the best characteristics of each constituent national group are enhanced and the worst portions are blocked through the interaction of diverse groups and the safeguards of democracy.

The personalities of different nations represent different parts of a perfect whole.

In America, older constraints and boundaries are removed. People's beliefs and attitudes are open to new concepts and opportunities. The characteristics and energies of diverse nationalities have created a dynamic national synergism. Because of this, America has been distinguished by the fairness and charity with which it has treated other nations. The allegiance of Americans to their former homelands has also contributed to this.

A nation, as represented by the collective actions of its people, is also accountable for its actions. Unfortunately, some nations may lose their fairness and evenhandedness and support the aggressor in some regional conflicts. As a result, it too may experience problems. The ultimate fate of a nation will be found in the manner it treats its neighbor and other nations. Good neighbor relations lead to mutual prosperity and growth. Dominance and the acquisition of a neighbor's land leads to hatred and loss for all parties involved.

Chapter 21

Democracy, Tyranny and War

Democracy

You may wonder why I am bringing up political issues in a spiritual discourse. Political ideologies, as well as religious extremism, have delayed or destroyed the spiritual development of countless people and have led to untold human grief. Your spiritual development is influenced by your political and social environment. Democracy is important to protect your spiritual development and prosperity.

Your spiritual development flourishes in freedom.

You are here to prosper in material things as well as in your soul and spirit. This is best achieved by the freedom of human initiative and enterprise. However, such enterprise must be tempered by checks and balances and the control of greed.

You are also responsible for the protection of the earth and its resources that I have given to you for your sustenance. I created the world for you. You are not a bystander or a byproduct of it. You are an active, not passive, participant in the care and management of its resources. Your choice of governance then is an important way to protect your material and spiritual development, and your home on earth. These goals are best assured by the checks and balances of a democratic government.

Freedom of human initiative and enterprise assure prosperity and spiritual growth.

Democracy is also vital for the competition of ideas and competing truths for your material and spiritual development. Mind control or any control of the freedom of thought or of the press must not be tolerated. There are many who are sufficiently insecure in their economic, social or religious dogmas that they seek to impose them on others.

I created the earth for you. You are not a by-product of it.

Beware of immoral and corrupt politicians. Their goal is power and domination and not your well being. They assume that their needs and values are superior to your own. I did not create you to be adversely affected or controlled by them.

Beware of dogmas and the self-righteous. Do not let anyone tell you how to live. I have witnessed a river of tears due to the cruelty of tyrannical governments. Resist those that block the human spirit and the development of its potential. Resist those who would squander the resources of your earth without care or regulation.

Resist those who through their dogmas block the human spirit and the development of its potential.

You must protect your democracy. Those who have lived under tyranny understand its critical importance. Do not take your freedom and liberty for granted. If you do not protect your freedom, you will lose it. Without checks and balances, the lesser among you can gain power and impose their tyranny upon you. The success of democracy depends upon leaders with competence, integrity and good character.

If you don't protect your freedom you will lose it.

Governmental control by religious groups should also be avoided. Those who presume to speak for God are anxious to impose their dogmas and narrow beliefs. I have given you judgment and ability to reason. Use them to protect yourselves and your freedom. Be vigilant and protect your spiritual heritage as a free person.

Do not be passive in your societies. Express your doubts and be outraged by the excesses of others that destroy your common home. Vote when you can. The will of the collective society can spontaneously impose change and unconsciously influence the will of its leaders. Let no one tell you how to live.

The success of democracy depends upon leaders with competence and integrity.

In addition to democracy and freedom, you cannot have prosperity without a high level of moral worth in the majority of your citizens. It is they who hold the fabric of your nation together and assure its functioning. It also depends upon an honest system of enforcement and integrity in your judicial system. It is not assured by the most educated or wealthy persons. It depends upon the enterprise and industry of persons of good character, who do not abuse the system, regardless of position or wealth.

Tyranny

Beware of communism, and other authoritarian governments, and those who deny and suppress freedom and religion. They admit and recognize no higher power than themselves. The intolerance and control that they impose in the name of social good, destroys personal initiative and creativity and impoverishes everyone. They naively think that they know better than you and can organize and dictate your life. Checks and balances are lost and corruption flourishes. Their proposed aims are "noble" but their results are disastrous. A welfare state creates economic and spiritual poverty. Unless you resist tyranny, political or religious, you will suffer under it. Democracy and economic freedom are the essential key to prosperity, your personal freedoms and personal development.

Those who deny you freedom are an affront to me. Those who deny their own spirit are an affront to themselves.

The presumed utopian goals of communism are actually achieved through free enterprise not government control and regulation. Communism as a totalitarian government destroys initiative and lacks the checks and balances found in democracies. Without such controls, the evil and greed of a few triumph and all suffer in the name of an asserted noble ideal. The "idealism" of a few destroys the quality of life for many. Each person deserves the fruits of their labor. Prosperity cannot be achieved on the backs of others.

Prosperity cannot be achieved on the backs of others.

Also be alert to the "potential pitfalls" of socialism. It is on a continuum to the right of communism. It can quickly shift to the left depending upon the existing social or political climate and political opportunity. Their professed value system is helping the poor and less fortunate, without justice or charity at their personal level. They find their morality in public policy issues. They need to control how others live and think. Radical socialists consider integrity an impediment to their goals. They will resort to any deception to achieve them.

"Socialist" minded individuals do not want self-reliance and initiative on your part. If their policies are adopted, it reassures their insecurities and doubts. It demonstrates to themselves and others that they are "caring" people. Like a "true believer," their lives achieve structure and security by adopting some dogma.

Socialists need the security and structure of their dogma.

To counter opposing views, they will limit or try to impede the freedom of speech. They thrive on a dependent rather than a self-reliant society. When in power, they will restrict or chip away at your freedom and economic opportunities. While they participate in a democratic society, they may undermine it when given the opportunity.

War

Nations that cannot live with each other, attack each other. The spiritual poverty of its leaders, embroil its people for national gain or power. Too often, their policies are embraced by their people. War is abhorred by me and all those who seek peace. However unjust, I gave you the capability to protect and defend yourselves and your homes against the aggressor..

He, who does not defend his home, does not deserve it.

War brings out the worst and best in mankind. It emboldens the worst persons to do evil deeds and brings out the best behavior in those of good character to protect their nation. In earlier times, battle was a way to develop character and discipline. It is a time of honor, duty, sacrifice and brotherhood. The good person does their duty and shows bravery. For this reason, they are usually the first to die. They test their mettle and are found to be worthy.

The individual and group challenges imposed by war lead to comradeship. Due to the sacrifices that people make for each other, more love is born in war than in peaceful times. Although unfortunate, those who die in war are only "fallen". Their valor is not lost. They dwell among their comrades. They will meet their loved ones again.

More love is born in war than in peace.

No soldier who dies in defense of his country dies in vain. They are honored in my presence. When they again return to earth, they will prosper in all of the blessings that they had freely forfeited in their young lives.

As people mature, the world, like you, is progressing and becoming a more harmonious whole. Despite the continuing carnage in the world, it is getting less as you learn to control your aggressions and live with your neighbors.

Chapter 22

Conclusion

W hy then are you here? What is the meaning of life? As part of me, you are here to develop your living and eternal spirit, to become one with me in love and to grow in spiritual value. Your living and eternal spirit interacts with every phase and aspect of your life. Your moral worth, and assured atonement for your negative deeds, explains every aspect and occurrence in your life.

Your moral worth, and assured atonement for your negative deeds, explains every aspect and occurrence in your life.

I expect you to be pro-active, to be assertive in life, to take control and to be a moral example for others. Live proud, be proud. You are here for a reason. Be alert to your spiritual needs and atone for your misdeeds. You are responsible for your own behavior.

You are responsible for your behavior.

To be passive in life and unaware of your spiritual being is to be buffeted by random forces beyond your control. The consequences of an ignored spirit are failure, unhappiness and an unfulfilled life. Those who do not recognize and accept my existence have a veil over their eyes. They will live vainglorious lives without true understanding and meaning.

Rejoice that I chose you for life! I chose you to be a part of me. Your attention, or lack of attention to your moral worth, will facilitate or hinder the quality of your life in this world and the next.

Resist any influence that can limit, retard or distort your personal development, spiritual growth, freedom, prosperity and happiness. Resist tyrannical governments and religious forces that are contrary to your best interests, judgment and instincts. Fight any injustice to yourself and others as a personal duty of your spiritual self. Resist perfidy of any kind. You are responsible for your actions and inactions. To remain morally passive in view of the opportunities and challenges I have given to you is a denial of your spirit.

To remain morally passive, in view of the opportunities and challenges that I have given to you, is a denial of your spirit.

Enjoy the journey that I have embarked you upon. Strive and persevere. I am with you and will not let you falter. As you have lived through me, I have lived through you. As you have loved me, I have loved you. Having loved you, would I abandon you in death? You are always in my presence and are eternal.

As you have loved me, I have loved you.

Fear not; through my love, you will not be harmed. You are not a victim. Your living spirit is eternal. Those of you who have completed their journey, and have achieved perfection, will reside in my presence for eternity. They are perfect souls. They too watch over you and intercede for me. They are my surrogates and are what you call angels.

Having loved you, would I abandon you in death?

As an eagle is lifted on currents of air, let your spirit soar on my love. As an eagle sees its reflection in the water, so does your spirit see itself in me. As the sun rises each morning, refresh your living and eternal spirit with faith, love and good will.

www.ingramcontent.com/pod-product-compliance
Lightning Source LLC
Chambersburg PA
CBHW031959080426
42735CB00007B/443